Dec. 26, 2008

DIVINING DIVINITY
A Book of Poems

BY JOSEPH PEARCE
WITH
ILLUSTRATIONS BY JEF MURRAY

Merry Christmas,
Fran + Pete!

Love,
Fran

• • •

A Dedicatory Whimsy
in Poor Taste
and Worse Grammar

I'm not averse
To amuse,
So here's a verse
To a muse!

CONTENTS

Prefatory Note

This volume of verse is dedicated to those of my superiors to whom its very existence is due. I refer to those poets and writers who have impregnated my unworthy Muse. It is indeed no exaggeration to say that every line of the verse that follows carries within it the unmistakable mark of one or other of those mentors of my imagination to whom I am indescribably indebted. I can, therefore, only in the loosest sense describe the verse that follows as my own. The real credit, under grace, belongs to the great princes of the imagination who were its inspiration. I would add, however, that although they may be responsible for this volume they are emphatically not to blame for it! Anything worthy of merit is theirs; the failings and defects are mine. Theirs is the inspiration; mine is merely the aspiration and perspiration. Theirs is the blood that gives life to this corpus of work; mine is the sweat; perhaps the tears are reserved for the reader!

At any rate, the princes of the imagination to whom I dedicate this volume are so many that I doubt that I could remember them all. Among the most important are Dante (obviously!), Hopkins, Sassoon, Belloc, Eliot, Francis Thompson, R.S. Thomas, George Herbert and St. John of the Cross. Other literary influences who have been very important, though perhaps not strictly in the poetic sense, are John Henry Newman, J.R.R. Tolkien, G.K. Chesterton and last, but indubitably not least, Shakespeare.

As for the volume's title it suggests that the poetry should be read in the realm of mystery, magic, miracle and metaphor. It cannot be read literally, on which level it is probably literally meaningless. As such, literalists and other materialists need not bother to read any further, not least because they do not really know how to read. There is, however, one poem at least which even the literalists might understand. I refer to "The Hedgehog", a piece of juvenilia that I wrote long before I learned to think metaphorically. It has no hidden meaning. It works on no level above and beyond the earthy, literal level on which the hedgehog itself resides. Like the hedgehog, and the materialist, it has its nose in the dirt and never looks to the stars. It has no point except the points on the hedgehog's back.

The rest of the poems all have a point, though I do not see the point of pointing them out. I will leave the reader to discover the point, and to divine the divinity, for himself, mindful nonetheless of Chesterton's wistful comment that it didn't matter how much he made the point of a story stick out like a spike the critics still managed to impale themselves very carefully on something else. Wishing to do nothing to impair the impaling, I invite the critic to turn the following pages at his own risk. As for my more discerning reader, I invite him simply to see the point.

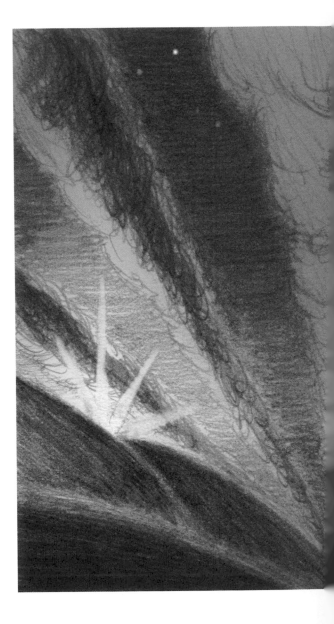

SOLSTICE SUNRISE

Deep in the dark night of the soul
Something stirs.
It is I,
Leaving dream's dreary hole
As morning stars
In summer sky.
And ere sun rises
From sleep to slumber
and dawning of dawn,
Alone one rises
In Lazarene lumber
to meet the morn.

And the world sleeps...

As gloaming fades
I stray and wander
In gladdening glades
to pray and ponder;
A voyeur visitor,
Impertinent impostor,
Inquisitive inquisitor,
Mumbling *Pater Noster*.
In stillness to stare
at solitary hare
that accompanies my prayer.

Does it know?
Is it waiting?
Is it, as I,
Anticipating?
It knows,
though what it knows,
It knows not:
Distinctive
but instinctive,
and oblivious
of oblivion.
Unconscious friar
in Franciscan fraternity;
the hare's breath

is the hair's breadth
from here to eternity.

And the world sleeps...

And as the hare
grassward grazes,
without a care
for heavenward gazes,
Something stirs.
Clouds clustered in pagan grey
Turn a mythic, mystic rose;
Heaven's heralds of the day,
Burning embers, amber glows.
Breeze through rushes,
shhhh, ...and hushes,
in silent awe at a maiden's blushes,
        Conceiving the Sun.
White, He rises
and soul surmises
resplendent disguises
        Concealing the One.

Corpus Christi!
Rising through the rose,
Sanguis Christi!
Skyward flows.

Heavenly Host
So new, so old,
As Holy Ghost
turns snow to gold.
Joy to Glory,
tinged with Sorrow,
Endless story,
new tomorrow.

Thus transfixed
in transient transfiguration,
the impressive impression
of mind's gaze
becomes expressive expression
and finds praise.
From deep draught of thought,
to prayer,
tasting sweet living water there,
Divining Divinity.

But there are none so blind,
(blinded by the night),
as they who will not see;
They neither seek nor find,
(though reminded by the light),
They are but will not be.

Yet as life exhales,
Passing the life sentence
through the Lamb's loam,
Love's exiles,
in repeated repentance,
long for Home.
And world's renunciation
wields annunciation,
Divining Divinity,
As choirs of angels
dressed as birds
sing songs of praise
too blessed for words
in finite
infinity.

And the world sleeps...

THE HEDGEHOG

I am a hedgehog,
In hedges I roam,
I eat mostly insects,
The shrubs are my home.
I'm a shapeless creature,
Hugging the ground,
And when people seek me
I am quickly found,
For rather than hide
I make myself round.

THE GRAMMAR OF ASSENT:
AN UNGRAMMATICAL ASCENT

*In this poem, the kernel of which came to me in a dream,
I have sacrificed grammar on the altar of rhyme.
The pedant, I hope, will forgive me.*

if Is,
is God?
if God,
is Christ?
if Christ,
is the Church?

questions
as Quest,
quest
as Bequest;
in Him
is Her
Inheritance.

you see,
says He,
the He
you see
is Me
in We,
and She
is He
in Me.

She,
you see,
was wooed
by We.

We wed,
We wedded
Her,
Flesh of Our Flesh,
Blood of Our Blood,
She
and We
are One.

We,
We One,
We won Her,
She
We won,
in wonder:
wonderful,
wonder-filled,
is She
in We,
and We
in She.

you see,
says He
to me;

you see
through me,
you see?

Through Me,
you See!

and who
are You?,
say I.

I am
Who am,
says He,
and you think
because
I am;

I am
Who am:
the Is
is Me,
and 'Me'
is He,
and He
is She.

... in We

11

DECONSTRUCTION

A *reductio ad absurdum*,
                    nihilistic negation
of everything
          to a primeval soup
                    of Nothing.

A minimalist trinity:
          sex and drugs and rock 'n' roll.

But even this trinitarian modernity
                    can be reduced...

Sex is merely a drug,
          and drugs and rock 'n' roll
                    merely a substitute for sex.

The new unity,
          the new unitarianism,
                    is sex...

Not Glorious Sex
          in its romantic heights
but gaudy sex
          in the furtive frustrations
                    of its sterile depths.

The omnipotence of impotence.

PREYER

Hell's faerie,
Fallen from grace,
The lords are with thee;
Abreast art thou among war men,
And blistered is the fruit of thy gloom,
Judas.
Hell of Melkor,
Mordor of dogs,
Preyer on us sinners
Now and at the hour
Of our deaths.

LOVE AND CUPID

I know I'm in love
But I don't thank Cupid,
Heavens above,
I'm not that stupid.

His amorous arrow
Can't find its mark,
His aim is too narrow,
His outlook too stark.

For love is a gift,
Given to me,
And now that it's mine
I give it to Thee.

COEUR DE LEAR'S CORDELIA

Midway through the darkened wood,
      the way unguessed,
Venturing forth from the
      sanctuary of the Shire,
To Rivendell where dreamy-spired
      dreams inspire,
I beheld a maiden from the mystic West.
Beguilèd by elven magic's majesty,
A new Arwen, Lúthien, Galadriel.
Laudate! A Elbereth Gilthoniel!
Beatrice, Penelope of my Odyssey!

Home is where the hearth is,
      and my heart's hearth's flame
Was kindled by her,
      my heart's hearth's home.
Coeur de Lear's Cordelia, love's lush loam,
Loved and was silent in Ilúvatar's name;
And when, in tunneled Time,
      Death do us part,
We'll still be together in His Sacred Heart.

DANTE DILETTANTE

Hope springs eternal on New Year's Day
Nineteen Fourteen,
And all sing *Auld Lang Syne*;
But Hell sings infernal songs
        (who hears, pray):
"Till 'a ye see's gangrene, my boys,
'A ye see's grangene,
And I will have ye here, my boys,
Where 'a ye see's gangrene."

Thus the red rose burns and has for thee
The subtle stench of blasphemy,
And bell's chime
Is Hell's crime
And the bell tolls for thee:
A virgin child,
So weak and wild,
A lamb to the slaughter;
Blinking blind,
Fumbling find
And kiss the devil's daughter;
A debutant dilettante,
Into Hell to follow Dante
And dance the deadly dance;
And so Sassoon,
So soon, Sassoon,
You join the necromance.

And not
In fear, no
Inferno
Story worries you.
Bland!
See no evil,
Speak no evil,
Infer no evil:
Glory hurries you.
Blind!

So they cheered as you marched to war,
A jingo jangled cavalier,
But sneered the sign above the door:
"Abandon hope who enters here."
And so Sassoon,
So soon, Sassoon,
In nightmare you're awake
With senseless insommeniacs,
Marneiacs, La Monsiacs,
A sight fair for a wake.

But the soldier is a mystic,
Foiling foolish fashion,
And redeemed and realistic,
Perceives poetic Passion;
And Siegfried freed
From Wagnerian curses

With sacred seed
Despair disperses.

Upsurge surgery!
Open heart purgery
Puts perjury to flight,
And purgatorial seeking,
Falsehood forsaking,
Finds paradismal light!

And so Sassoon,
So soon, Sassoon,
You lurch triumphant,
And find the key
To liberty
From the search circumferent.

And as you turn the key
You learn to see
That it unlocks
The paradox
Of Paradise.

The chance to cease
Life's labour's test,
He grants you Peace,
Ite, missa est.

KNEELING STONE

Space is merely Euclid's box,
Relatively tiny,
Theoretically speaking,
And pierced with holes
So that the spirits
Trapped within
Can breathe
       the breath of light.

And light,
Snail-like,
Sneaks up on us
Across the void;
No longer the king of speed
But a dethroned loiterer
Trapped within
And hanging upon
       the wyrd-woven web.

So,
naked,
one stone
kneels
before
the Rock.

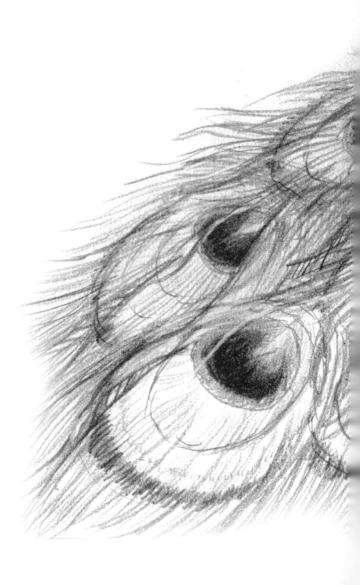

HOPKINS

One greater than
Donne scatters
Duns Scotus
And reaps reward.

MOTHEMATICS

Enwombed and warm
Amid firelit spark,
Out of the storm,
Away from the dark;

And out of the window,
Flocking in violence,
Moth upon moth
Knocking in silence.

Out in the tempest,
Barred from the shelter,
Butterflutter,
Helter skelter.

Fluttered
With no chance of winning,
Flustered
With no power of sinning;
Blameless,
Shameless,
Utterly aimless;
Instant, insistent instincts homing
In on the glow from out of the gloaming;

Flapping their part in symmetry fearful,
But oblivious to this mothematics,
Against the invisible barrier tearful
In obdurate, obstinate acrobatics.

Thence philosophical fluttering
For seeking light
And mystical muttering
Forsaking night.

I thought.

I sought.

Three score years and ten...
And then?

Glad glimpses of sad tidings,
Moth and man enshrined,
Parallel paraglidings,
Eternally entwined.

A wilderness
Of desert's dust,
A worlderness
of deserts just.

The wind of pain,
Of pain of breath,
The window pane
'Tween life and death!

And out of doom's erection,
Night's nightmare,
Came a resurrection
In form of prayer,

That night's neurosis
May shatter death's pane,
And the world's halitosis
Be fresh breath again.

Lands of shadow,
Shadowlands of gloom,
Smash the pane barrier
And lead me home.

Sing the herald angels, hark!,
A lilting lullabye, litany of light,
And clear the many dangers dark
That I may have eternal sight.

Sunrise, Sunset

Whenever the Catholic
      sun doth shine,
There's always laughter
      and good red wine.
At least I've always found it so.
Benedicamus Domino!

   – Hilaire Belloc

But when the Catholic sun doth sink,
There's stench of Hitler, Stalin's stink.
We hate to say we told you so.
Gulag Archipelago!

   – JP (with apologies to HB)

BELLOC

Not the bombast of relativism,
The bombast of mere opinion,
Sanitized by self-righteousness;
But the bombast of absolutes,
The bombast of certitude,
Sanctified by servitude
To the righteousness beyond the self.

THE BISHOP AND THE VIRGIN

The Bishop rose in the West,
The most famous celt of all;
And the Faith devoutly was confessed
From Cork to Donegal.

But the Virgin sank in the East,
Though risen from the Fall,
And though all of England
                   knows her least,
She is worthier than them all.

Patrick preached on Irish sod
The shamrock One-in-Three,
He turned the pagan gaels to God,
Till they all were one in Thee.

Withburga, princess pure and saint,
Daughter of a Saxon rex;
East Anglian wholly without taint,
Iconic image of her sex.

Patrick's Day is celebrated
In manners quite obscene,
By men whose faith is mutilated
In forty shades of green.

Withburga's Day is now forgotten,
As indeed is she,
By England turned rancid and rotten,
Footloose, fancy and unfree.

As Patrick is remembered
By policemen in New York,
And policemen are dismembered
By rebels from Dundalk,

I remember England,
Merrie, goode and free,
And March Seventeenth
Is Withburga's Day to me.

A Husband's Prayer

A song I'll sing of mothering,
And fathering, and sanctity,
And also sin, that other thing,
Which, dark and grim, offendeth Thee.
The song I sing is but a prayer
That I may grow in love and grace,
And, seeing sin as Satan's snare,
That I may know a husband's place;

And heal her heart that sins hath torn,
And bless her head that it may wear
A halo not a crown of thorn,
And saintly kiss caress her hair.
This is the desire of my dirge:
To be her knight and not her scourge

SUNSET

When Britain had an Empire
The sun would never set,
But the sun set over England
And Englishmen forget

That greater than the Empire
Are the rolling Yorkshire moors,
And more glorious the Dales
Than all the Empire's wars.